GO BACK AND GET IT!

Reclaiming My Life, My Dreams and My Freedom through Sankofa

MARCIA M. SPENCE

Go Back and Get It!

Reclaiming My Life, My Dreams, and My Freedom through Sankofa

By Marcia M Spence

© 2025 Marcia M Spence

ISBN 978-1-0681515-0-7

All rights reserved.

No part of this publication may be reproduced, stored in a retrieval system, or transmitted in any form or by any means, electronic, mechanical, photocopying, recording, or otherwise, without the prior written permission of the copyright owner, except with brief quotations embodied in critical articles and reviews.

This book is a work of nonfiction.

Scripture quotes are from the NIV and ESV Bibles.

First Edition, 2025

www.marciampublishing.com

DEDICATION

This book is dedicated to:

My children and grandchildren, who have given my life endless meaning, laughter, and love.

To the woman I used to be, who survived what was meant to break her.

To the woman I am now, who chose to heal, to thrive, and to live again.

And above all,
To God,
my unfailing refuge, my healer, my source, who held me through every storm and led me back to myself.

This is for you.
This is for us.
This is for every soul who still believes in a second beginning.

ACKNOWLEDGMENTS

I am deeply grateful for every soul who stood by me when self-reliance failed me.

To the one who believed me when others doubted.

To the counsellors and healers who guided me back to wholeness.

To every support group, every mentor, every author whose words kept my hope alive.

To my clients and readers who honour truth and resilience.

To my family, your love is my legacy.

To the little girl inside me, thank you for never giving up on me.

And most of all, to my Heavenly Father, who never left me, even when I felt most lost.

PREFACE

At 56 years old, I made a decision that changed everything.

After living for nearly a decade in the shadow of chronic illnesses, struggling to hold on to a sense of purpose, identity, and faith.

I finally looked backwards, not with regret, but with intention.

Failure upon failure, in business and relationships, along with the illusion of success, led me to this place.

I re-discovered the ancient Ghanaian principle of Sankofa, which teaches us that "*it is not wrong to go back and fetch what you have forgotten.*"

It gave me permission, and a roadmap, to reclaim the parts of myself I thought I had lost forever.

This book, **Go Back and Get It,** is not just about my journey through illness, grief, and rediscovery.

It is a celebration of what becomes possible when we dare to reach into our past, gather the dreams and passions we left behind, and weave them into the lives we are living now.

Reclaim what is yours; it is never too late.

This book is not a memoir. I wrote my full story in *Geraldines Pearl* (2016). This is a synopsis of my experiences and the lessons which helped me to stand strong, with clarity and power.

"Greatness is not found in fearing the past, but in loving the lessons it gave you, and walking boldly into your future."

ABOUT SANKOFA

Sankofa is a powerful principle from the Akan people of Ghana, West Africa.

It teaches that in order to move forward with wisdom, we must sometimes look back, to reclaim the treasures, lessons, and dreams we may have forgotten, lost, or set aside.

The word "Sankofa" comes from the Akan language:
San — to return
Ko — to go
Fa — to fetch, to seek, to retrieve.

It is often symbolised by a bird walking forward, while turning its head backward to gently retrieve a precious egg from its past. Or by a graceful, spiralling heart symbol — honouring love, heritage, and connection.

Sankofa reminds us:

- Healing does not mean erasing the past.
- Growth does not mean forgetting where we come from.
- True progress honours both the wounds and the wisdom of our journey.

In my own life, Sankofa became a lifeline.

When chronic illness, loss, and heartbreak seemed to break me, it was the act of looking back, with love, not shame, that saved me.

It was by reaching back into my childhood passions, my early strength, my buried dreams, I could move forward into a new life.

This book, this journey, this healing, is a living Sankofa.

And it is my hope that as you walk with me through these pages, you will begin your own Sankofa journey too, reclaiming everything beautiful, powerful, and sacred that has always been yours.

**GO BACK.
GET IT.
LIVE IT.**

CONTENTS

Preface 5

About Sankofa 7

Part One: Before the Storm 12

    Chapter 1: Roots of Passion 13

    Chapter 2: The Building Years 16

    Chapter 3: Building My Career 20

    Chapter 4: The Spark 25

    Chapter 5: Love Life 28

Part Two: When Life Changes Everything 32

    Chapter 6: Losing My Anchor, Finding My Wings 33

    Chapter 7: The Onset of Chronic Illness 37

    Chapter 8: Money and Me 39

    Chapter 9: Faith is My Anchor 43

    Chapter 10: What Pain Taught Me 46

    Chapter 11: In The Wilderness 50

Part Three: The Turning Point 52

    Chapter 12: Whispers from the Past 53

    Chapter 13: Learning About Sankofa 54

    Chapter 14: A New Era 56

    Chapter 15: The Catalyst 60

Chapter 16: Walking the Sankofa Path 68

Chapter 17: No Regrets: A Lesson in Acceptance 72

Chapter 18: The Gift of Pace and Being Still 75

Chapter 19: The Power of Intuition 79

Chapter 20: This Is Not About Other People 82

Chapter 21: Legacy in Motion 84

Part Four: For the Reader: Your Sankofa Journey 87

Chapter 22: Lessons Learned Along the Way 88

Chapter 23: Womanhood Sacred, Sensual, and Seen 90

Chapter 24: Dreaming of My Soft Girl Era 96

Chapter: 25: My Dilemma 100

Chapter 26: A Call to Action, Start Your Sankofa Journey 104

Chapter 27: It Is Never Too Late 106

***Closing Reflection:* You Come First** 108
Your Go Back and Get It Journey 110
Your Journey Continues 139
About the Author 151
Part Five: Continuing Your Journey 153

Ready to Continue Your Journey? 154

Bonus Chapters Crucial Wisdom Gained through Sankofa! 161

Bonus Chapter Building While Breaking The Birth of a Publishing House 162

Bonus Chapter Curating Peace in a Social World.......... 167

Bonus Chapter The Long Road to Patience and Forgiveness... 171

Bonus Chapter The Pieces of Me Motherhood and Grandmotherhood 175

Part One:
BEFORE THE STORM

"You were never meant to live shackled by the fear of what has been.

You were meant to live empowered by the love of what you have survived.

Your past does not define your limits — it reveals your strength.

Greatness is already yours to claim."

Chapter 1:
ROOTS OF PASSION

Before life taught me about pain, about slowing down, about starting over. I lived with a fire inside me, a steady, bright fire of dreams and ambitions. I was full of energy, creativity, and a sense of possibility. I always believed that with hard work, love, and determination, anything was possible.

I learned early that a house may be a dangerous place. I was incredibly young when I learned what violence sounded like. By age nine, I'd relocated countless times. Seven schools. Seven fresh starts. Each move was another desperate attempt by my mother to outrun the man who claimed he loved us but hurt us, anyway.

I learned to creep, to keep my bag half-packed, to let go of friends and toys without tears. Home was no longer a place. It turned into wherever my mother found a locked door and a little quiet.

Inside the wreckage, I refused to be swallowed whole.

School became my battleground and my safe place all at once. I was quick, bright, stubborn. I devoured books like they were food and sneaking them under the covers with a torch when nightmares wouldn't let me sleep. Between the pages, I found places where girls like me fought back. Where monsters lost. Where homes stayed safe and children could just be children.

I danced at every opportunity. I sang as if my voice would drown out the screaming from my memories. I ran faster than everyone else, kicked footballs harder, laughed louder. Every gold star stuck to my homework, every prize ribbon from a race, every applause after a school play. It was all a way of saying; *You won't break me.*

But the shadows were never far behind.

There were things I didn't talk about. Things that happened when adults thought no one would notice. Moments that left a stain inside me, silent and sticky, a weight too big for a child to carry. I buried them deep, wrapped them up in silence, thinking if I didn't say the words out loud, maybe they'd no longer harm me.

Some days, the memories caught up with me, anyway. The echoes of anger made me want to disappear. But I didn't.

I couldn't do that!

I learned to survive by building worlds inside myself, worlds of music, dance, games, books. Worlds where I wasn't the girl with the anxiety or the secrets. Worlds where I was just Marcia, and that was enough.

I relied on me; I felt safe alone, in my world, in my fantasies, in my creative space. I discovered that anything I tried; I was good at it, everything.

Life transitions destabilised me, leading to self-doubt. I coped with grief and trauma by focusing on achievement, finding joy in learning and school.

By nine years old, I was fighting back, with every step I danced, every word I read, every breath I took.

The world had tried to shatter me.

But I was still standing.

And I was just getting started.

Chapter 2:
THE BUILDING YEARS

I fell in love like someone who had been starving all her life.

I was still a teenager, only 15 full of hope and longing, when I first felt it, that deep, aching hunger to be seen, held, and cherished. Growing up, I hadn't known the steady, protective love of a father. I had watched the damage a man could do to a woman; I had also felt the icy sting of a father figure who couldn't love me as I needed. I felt overlooked and unimportant.

My mother shielded us with everything she had. She was strong, and full of love, the kind of mother I aspired to be one day.

Still, somewhere deep inside, there was a space that longed to be filled. A muted emptiness left by the absence of a close, safe bond with a man.

So, when he looked at me like I mattered, when he spoke to me with warmth and tenderness, it felt like stepping into the sunlight after a long, frosty winter.

He was kind, charming, and full of promises. He made me feel special, chosen, loved. I wanted a fresh start. I wanted to build the family where laughter filled the rooms, where love stayed and didn't hurt. I was young and hopeful, and that felt like enough.

We moved quickly, riding the thrill of adolescent love. I wore the wedding dress, trembling with excitement. I said my vows with a heart bursting with dreams. We set up home with second-hand furniture and big plans for the future. We had children, two beautiful, bright-eyed children, and I poured my heart into being a mother, just like the one who had fought so hard for me.

I read to them, sang to them, cooked meals, made birthdays magical. I wanted their childhoods to be rich with the kind of love I knew a mother could give.

I loved them and I loved him; I did not know I had to love myself too; I thought love was to be given away to others. Love was certainly not for me.

We were happy, I thought, life was good.

But underneath it all, something was wrong. I could feel it, a slow, creeping coldness seeping into the life we were building.

It started small. Unexplained absences, strange moods that swung from silence to fury, nights when he wouldn't sleep, pacing and muttering. I dismissed it as the stress of early parenthood: too many bills, too little time. We were both still in our twenties, too young, it seemed, but still full of fight.

Then the truth began to show itself.

He was sick. Severely mentally ill. Worse still, he was slipping into addiction, using drugs I didn't even know how to name. The man I married faded into a ghost of himself, unreachable, unrecognisable.

The life we had built together falling apart piece by piece.

I tried to hold on, for the children, for the promises we had made, for the version of him I had once loved. I hid the worst of it behind closed doors. I made excuses, carried the weight of it on my back, the way women often do when they believe they can love someone enough to save them.

But it was too big, too broken.

Go Back and Get it

The fights grew louder. Money disappeared. Trust shattered. Our home, once filled with hope, became a place of tension and fear, a battlefield of a different kind.

And I saw my children looking at me with wide, confused eyes, just as I had once looked at my mother.

By the time I finally walked away, the children were still so little, both under nine years old. I carried them out of that wrecked life, just like my mother had once carried us, determined to protect them at any cost.

I wasn't the same girl who had fallen in love blindly.
I was scarred! Wiser and fiercer.

And this time, I vowed: I would never lose myself again, not for love, not for hope, not for anyone.

Chapter 3:
BUILDING MY CAREER

I started working at fifteen, a Saturday girl stacking shelves and serving customers at a freezer food shop. It lacked glamour, yet it meant the world to me. It signified independence. It was a way to carve out a life for myself on my own terms. Every Saturday morning, I pulled on my uniform, showed up on time, and worked hard, small steps on a path I was determined to build myself.

At seventeen, I took another step forward and joined a Youth Training Scheme (YTS), working and training as a Travel Clerk for a chain of travel agencies. It felt exciting to be part of something bigger, to learn skills that opened doors into the world of business and travel. I loved the rhythm of it, booking holidays, talking to customers about places I had only dreamed of visiting. It gave me a glimpse of possibility, of how far I could go if I worked hard enough.

I stayed until I had my first baby at nineteen. Becoming a mother changed everything, but it didn't change my ambition. If anything, it sharpened it. I knew I wanted to build something stronger, something lasting, for both me and my child.

By nineteen, I had shifted my focus to community work and play-work, pouring my energy into helping children and families thrive. It felt natural to be part of something that lifted others up. Maybe because I knew, firsthand, what it felt like to need someone who cared. I loved it, the energy, the creativity, the purpose.

At twenty, I made a bold move: I started setting up community enterprises. No safety nets, no guarantees, just vision, passion, and the will to create opportunities where there were none. I organised services for women and children, creating spaces where safety and hope were not luxuries but basics we all deserved.

Every project I started, every group I supported, stitched itself into the fabric of the community, and into me. During this time, at 21, I gave birth to my second child, a girl, a beautiful bright-eyed daughter.

Those early years taught me that leadership wasn't about titles or pay grades. It was about courage. It was about seeing a need and deciding you were the one to answer it.

Home life was hectic, football on Tuesdays and Thursdays, matches on Sundays, swimming, and singing lessons for my daughter. After a full day's work, I became the taxi driver, the cheerleader, the provider.

Step by step, opportunity by opportunity, I built a career I could be proud of. I learned not just how to lead, but how to listen. How to create change that lasted longer than a single project or programme. By the age of thirty-six, I had risen to become a Senior Strategic Manager for my local council. Leading complete systems of support for some of the most vulnerable people in the borough.

Sitting at those senior tables, I carried everything with me, from the freezer shop, the travel desk, battered play centres. Also, the grassroots groups trusted me, even when I was very young. I never forgot where I came from. I never forgot who I was doing it for.

Alongside building my career, I kept studying, pushing myself harder and further. I knew passion and instinct would only take me so far; I needed the knowledge and the credentials. I studied leadership, social work, community development, and management, eventually rising to master's level.

It wasn't easy. I juggled raising children, leading services, and attending university lectures after long days at work. But every essay, every lecture, every exhausted late night was another brick laid in the foundation of my future.

My career wasn't handed to me. Graft, faith, stubbornness, and an unshakeable belief in a brighter future built it.

From stacking shelves to selling travel dreams, to changing lives on the ground and at the strategy table, every step mattered.

I didn't just build a career.

I built a life.

Though young and inexperienced, I was determined.
Even when my personal life crumbled, I kept building. I focused on building a career and a home for my children. I then had three children, another daughter as a single woman.

But success was never far from me. Each child I gave birth to led to career advancement.

After the birth of my son, the first child, I moved into community, play, and childcare. Whilst carrying my second child, I managed community projects. After the birth of my third I took over running a day nursery.

The roles I played in the community, the authority I held, led to me being disliked and misinterpreted. I held enormous responsibility at a young age. This caused some disconnect with my peers. I was no longer interested in chilling or socialising. I had purpose and I was on a mission. I was also holding on for dear life as I juggled single parenthood.

I recall the day I was at home at 36 years old; the children were three, fifteen and seventeen, and received the phone call.

I had been offered a Programme Manager position, after being rejected for a Deputy Manager role.

Not only was this a major career breakthrough, but it came with a £9,000 pay rise.

I stood there with tears in my eyes, proud of what I had achieved through perseverance.

This position was a game changer. I was ready to rise.

My joy was overwhelming. I had proved my worth. I could provide and we, as a family, could thrive.

Chapter 4:
THE SPARK

Men came and went, one giving me my third child. But they didn't stay, and honestly, I didn't want them to. I persevered, creating, nurturing, building. The longing for love remained there, tucked in the back of my heart, but it never stopped me from pouring love into my children and my dreams.

I raised my three children, two from my marriage and one from a later relationship, alone. Their fathers played their role within their own capacity. I had loved both men in separate ways, at different times in my life. But love alone wasn't enough to hold us together. Our dreams faded because of problems we couldn't solve and diverging paths.

When my third child was born, there was a vast twelve-year gap between her and my second. I was also single. Life reset itself. I had a toddler and teenagers juggling the challenges of both ages.

It felt like two lives: parenting a baby and near-adult children in a risky environment.

Gang culture had a forceful grip on the streets then. It appealed to young men, promising brotherhood, protection, and respect. For a time, my older children struggled under the pressure. Good kids, strong kids, but still vulnerable to the voices of the street.

I cannot put into words the fear that lived in my chest during those years. A constant tightness, a gnawing dread every time the phone rang late at night, or a siren screamed in the distance. I was constantly exhausted from work and family responsibilities.

There were days when I felt shattered, stretched thin between work meetings, school runs, sleepless nights, and the constant fear that my child might not return home one day.

I turned to the only place I knew could hold me when nothing else could: God.

Prayer became my anchor. Fasting became my weapon. Day and night, I prayed for my children, sometimes whispering, sometimes weeping, sometimes yelling. I submitted them to God's care, acknowledging paths beyond my reach and dangers I could not prevent, however much I wished otherwise.

I clung to faith because the surrounding reality often felt too bleak to bear.

Things shifted through grace and relentless love. My children found their way back. They remembered who they were. They chose life over the death the streets offered. The process proved arduous, yet they persevered.

I made it through.

We made it through.

Juggling toddler, teen, and work was a constant balancing act. Moments of madness threatened to overwhelm me. But somehow, God made a way through it all.

He strengthened me when I had nothing left. He covered my children when my arms couldn't reach. He turned my mourning into dancing, even when it took years to hear the music again. Hindsight reveals a beautiful tapestry woven from prayer, struggle, and perseverance.

I was not perfect. I made mistakes. But I worshipped, I battled, and I refused to give up.

And by God's grace, we survived and we rose.

Chapter 5:
LOVE LIFE

I have never had a problem finding a man. Throughout my life, meeting men, catching their interest, wasn't the issue. The problem was deeper, quieter, stitched into parts of me I hadn't understood. I seemed to attract, or accept, men who were not good for me. Men who didn't love me the way I deserved to be loved. Men who couldn't or wouldn't commit to building a life side by side, heart to heart.

Looking back, I see now that it wasn't because I wasn't worthy. It was because somewhere inside me, despite all my achievements, despite the accolades, the promotions, the degrees, I still carried the belief that I wasn't enough. That I was the bad one, as I was labelled in childhood. I was broken through divorce, unworthy of being chosen.

The mirror reflected not just my body but every cruel word that had ever been spoken over me.

"You're scary."
"You're not soft enough."
"You're not shapely enough."

I grew up hearing these things, sometimes from the very mouths that were supposed to love and protect me. I struggled with my body confidence from my 20s; I developed this after having postnatal depression; I lost all confidence. The words were like invisible scars, no matter how outwardly strong I appeared.

So, I overcompensated.
I was capable.
I was loving, nurturing, attentive.
I built beautiful homes, created safe spaces, and managed finances with skill. I poured myself into being the kind of woman any man would be lucky to have.

And yet, repeatedly, I chose men who couldn't meet me where I stood.

Men who said I was "too powerful" for them.

Men who admired my strength but resented it at the same time.

Men who took what I offered but rarely gave back.

I held ambitious standards for myself and for those around me. I believed if I fulfilled my side of the bargain, they would too. But often, they didn't. I ended up carrying the weight of the relationship, giving more than I should, accepting less than I needed.

It took me many years to understand the truth: I accepted toxicity because I had not yet healed the deep wounds of my past. Toxic and damaged men were who I was used to. They were familiar to me.

I was still searching for love and belonging, but often, I was looking at the wrong people. Thinking no one better would accept me.

I thought if I could just be good enough, kind enough, successful enough, beautiful enough, someone would finally choose me, stay with me, value me.

I thought love could fix what was broken.

But love, genuine love, doesn't demand that you change your shape to fit someone else's empty spaces.

Genuine love holds you as you are, powerful and imperfect and whole.

The healing has been slow, painful, messy. It has meant turning inward instead of outward. It has meant learning that my worth is not something another person can give me or take away.

It has meant understanding that I am already enough.

I no longer settle for being someone's second thought.
I no longer apologise for my power or shrink myself to make others comfortable.
I am learning fiercely to choose myself first.

Not because I have given up on love.

But because genuine love begins here, within me.

And the next time romantic love finds me, it will have to meet me where I stand, strong, whole, and finally, finally knowing my worth.

Part Two:
WHen LiFe CHANGES EVERYTHING

"To live in love, not fear, is to gather the broken pieces of your past and build a future more beautiful than you ever imagined."

Chapter 6:
LOSING MY ANCHOR, FINDING MY WINGS

When my grandmother died in 2011, it felt like the ground cracked beneath my feet.

She wasn't just my elder. She was my closest friend, my ally, my confidant. She understood parts of me that no one else could reach; the parts shaped by things too heavy to say aloud. Her presence in my life was like a lighthouse, steady and unwavering, guiding me through storms I often had to face alone.

I had already been grieving for years before she passed. My mother, my first home, and anchor had moved abroad to start a new chapter of her life. Although I was proud of her bravery, the distance left an ache inside me. I never quite learned to silence. That loss made me cling to my grandmother even harder. I needed her voice, her stories, her prayers, her sheer, unshakeable faith that no matter how terrible things looked, we would find a way through.

When she died, I didn't think I would survive it.

Outwardly, I was still strong, still capable. People looked at me and saw a woman who could juggle a career, raise a family, and stand up in rooms full of leaders without blinking. But inside, I was hollowed out. Vulnerable in ways that scared even me.

In that vulnerable place, aching for belonging and comfort, I fell into a marriage inside the church. I wanted safety. I wanted to believe that someone could step in and help me carry the weight. But love built on brokenness is never safe.

The relationship was abusive, controlling, suffocating and damaging. It didn't take long for me to realise that if I stayed, I would lose myself. I had survived too much, fought too hard to let that happen.

So, I got out, swiftly, quietly, with as much dignity as I could muster.

All I could do was cling to my faith.

Losing my grandmother broke me open.

But it also forced me to grow.

She would have been proud, I think, not because everything turned out neatly, but because I refused to stay small. Because I kept believing there could still be more.

Even now, I carry her strength inside me, the quiet, stubborn belief that no matter how rough the road gets, I can find my way through.

And I am still finding it.

And then, with everything in pieces around me, I made the boldest decision of my life: I left my job. I stepped away from the secure, familiar world I had built for decades. I chose freedom, even though it terrified me.

I didn't know where I was going, but I knew what I couldn't do anymore, live inside walls that suffocated my spirit.

I began a journey into entrepreneurship, into creativity, into possibilities I hadn't dared to explore when I was busy surviving. I wrote. I created. I built. I failed. I learned. I kept going.

The last thirteen years have been some of the hardest of my life.

Income dropped. Opportunities dried up. The weight of uncertainty felt almost unbearable. There were moments I questioned whether I had made a terrible mistake, giving up security for a dream that seemed so fragile, so impossible at times.

But even through all the testing, through the loss, the loneliness, and the fear, I have never regretted choosing freedom.

I have discovered pieces of myself I would never have known if I had stayed in the places that tried to shrink me. I have found resilience I didn't know I had, faith I didn't know I would need, creativity that had been buried under years of responsibility.

One step, one dream, one breath at a time.

Chapter 7:
THE ONSET OF CHRONIC ILLNESS

While I was soaring in my entrepreneurship and family life, another storm was gathering silently, inside my body.

It began with what I thought was a simple toothache.

Severe pain gripped me, keeping me awake for nights on end.

Living then with my youngest daughter, I endured emergency dentist visits where they told me, "Your teeth are perfect."

So why this excruciating pain?

After months of suffering and investigation, I was diagnosed with Trigeminal Neuralgia –
a condition so brutal it's often called "the suicide disease."

Every breath, every whisper of wind, became agony.

For three long months, I couldn't work.
I could barely speak or eat.
Depression crept in, heavy and dark.
My nervous system was shot.

When the right medication finally eased the worst of it, I thought perhaps I could live normally again.

But life had another twist:

Four years later, after working full time for myself and trying to stay active, my fingers started tingling after gym sessions.

This time, after more tests, I was diagnosed with Fibromyalgia.

Chronic fatigue.
Chronic pain.
Another thief in my life, one that couldn't be seen, but stole everything.

Chapter 8:
MONEY AND ME

When I was young, money mattered to me, not because I loved it, but because I understood what it could do.

Money meant freedom. Money meant security. Money meant giving my children the life I had always dreamed of a life where they didn't just survive but thrived. I wanted them to have their needs met and their dreams nourished. Experiences like music lessons, school trips, and holidays; plus, enough food, clothes, and a good education. I wanted to show them a life that stretched beyond what the world expected from a lone-parent household.

I took pride, a deep, fierce pride, in knowing that I provided all of it myself. My career, my determination, my careful planning, it was all for them.

When I left my job, I walked away with a comfortable payout. I didn't plunge into a financial struggle. For a time, there was breathing space, a chance to explore entrepreneurship, creativity, and possibility. I kept providing, kept dreaming.

When my health collapsed, and with it, my financial stability.

The struggle with money didn't creep. It stormed in.
I fell into debt.
I fell behind on my mortgage.

Sometimes buying food became an anxious calculation rather than a given.

My inability to support my children, as I always had, crushed me. Not being able to say yes when they needed something small, something meaningful. I grieved not just for the money, but for the part of me that had built her identity on being the provider, the strong one, the anchor.
Yet even in those dark years, I never stopped serving.

Despite my personal financial struggles, I built a business that gave other people opportunities. I earned little, but my business gave jobs to many. This boosted my clients' finances, social standing, and careers. I gave my all. I served. I didn't take; I poured into others, even when I had so little left for myself.

But there was another layer to my struggle. I had spent so many years running community services in salaried roles that in running my business; I found being *commercial* difficult. Charging for my work felt uncomfortable. It felt almost like "money grabbing," even when I knew I was giving and giving.

My heart was still wired for service, but service without proper boundaries quickly became sacrifice, and it was a sacrifice I could no longer afford to make.

Holding onto my dignity was paramount. Outwardly, no one would have known the battles I fought behind closed doors. That was my quest during those years of sickness: to conceal my suffering, but to stand publicly with grace and strength.

Ironically, when I was employed, I had never been shy about asking for what I was worth.

I studied hard, pursued qualifications, sought promotions and bigger salaries.
I understood my value, and I demanded it.

But when I became vulnerable, when illness took my strength, I lost the energy, and somewhere along the way, the self-belief, to champion my own financial interests.

I served for little.
I gave discounts.
I offered free support, thinking somehow it would come back to me with goodwill.

Instead, I learned a brutal truth:
Those who paid the least often showed the least respect.

The kindness I offered became an invitation for disrespect.
And as I healed, I saw it clearly.

No more.

The woman who once fought for her value has returned wiser, harder, sharper.

I now know that generosity must have boundaries. That service must not cost your dignity. That your gifts deserve to be honoured, not exploited.

I may have struggled.
I may have fallen.

But I have also risen, with the fierce understanding that I am worth more than the world once tried to convince me.
And this time, I will not sell myself short.

Chapter 9:
FAITH IS MY ANCHOR

My faith is not something I simply speak about; it is the force that holds me together.

I am a Christian woman with a deeply personal relationship with God. Not just religion, not just tradition, but a connection rooted in love, grace, and divine guidance. Jesus Christ is my Saviour. He walks with me, talks with me, comforts me, and calls me forward when I forget who I am.

There have been many times in my life when things made little sense. When I was in pain. When the tears fell. When my body was frail and my soul was weary. But even in the depths, I could feel God's hand not removing every obstacle but steadying me through each one.

The truth is, I stray. We all do. There are times when I've tried to manage things in my own strength, when I've run ahead, or pulled away. But I always return. Because He never left.

I think often about **Psalm 139**, where David writes, *"Where can I go from your Spirit? Where can I flee from your presence? If I go up to the heavens, you are there; if I make my bed in the depths, you are there."*

This scripture reminds me that even in the places where I feel lost, broken, or unsure, God is present. Not in condemnation, but in compassion. He sees the whole of me, the strong woman and the soft-hearted daughter. The fighter and the one who weeps. And He still calls me His own.

There is a kind of safety in that. A knowing. A spiritual security that I cannot find anywhere else.

When I was navigating chronic illness, the medical system failed me more than once. But God didn't. When I faced grief, betrayal, or loneliness, it was His presence that held me, not with loud miracles, but with daily bread. Peace for today. Strength for the next step.

He has provided. He has sent help. He has opened doors I could never force and closed doors I didn't understand until later. And time after time, He has whispered, *"You are mine."*

That is the foundation of everything I do – in my writing, my business, my coaching, my healing. I do not move without seeking His direction. And even when I get it wrong, He redirects me with love.

God is not just in my Sunday worship. He is in my work, my rest, my boundaries, my purpose, and my becoming. I am a woman of faith, not because I have all the answers, but because I have *the anchor*. And even when the storms rage, I will not be moved.

Because I know in whom I believe.
And I know that He is faithful.

Chapter 10:
WHAT PAIN TAUGHT ME

Pain has been one of my greatest teachers, though not one I ever wanted.

It crept in at first, stealing small pieces of my life before I even realised what was happening.

It started in my face, sharp, stabbing, electric bolts of agony that tore through my days and haunted my nights. I lived with that pain daily, learning to smile through it, work through it, parent through it.

Then, in 2019, the pain spread.

No longer contained, it became global, my whole-body aching, burning, protesting even the simplest movements. Pain became the backdrop to my life, louder than my thoughts, stronger than my willpower.

When pain is at its peak, nothing else exists.
There is no ambition.

No dream.

No conversation.

No tomorrow.

There is only pain.

It took from me without apology.

It isolated me, separated me from people, from experiences, from the very rhythms of the life I had built.

I was so humiliated that simple things like phone calls, dressing, cooking, walking, or driving became overwhelming.

It forced me to cancel plans, to apologise for things that weren't my fault, to stand at the edges of gatherings pretending I wasn't barely holding on.

Pain froze parts of my life in place.

Dreams and aspirations I had nurtured were suddenly put on hold, not because I lacked drive or vision, but because my body could not carry them forward.

It is a strange thing, to be full of passion, ideas, and fire, and yet to be trapped in a body that cannot always keep up.

Pain stripped away the illusions I once held about strength.

Strength, I learned, is not smiling when everything hurts.

Strength is allowing yourself to grieve the life you thought you would have.

Strength is accepting what is real while still fighting to create what can be.

In those long hours of isolation, when the world moved on without me, pain taught me patience.
Not the kind you preach about, but the kind you wrestle with, sob through, grit your teeth against.

Pain taught me humility, the kind that makes you drop to your knees and admit that you cannot do everything alone.

It taught me compassion for others who suffer, for those whose battles are invisible but no less fierce.

Pain taught me to listen, to my body, to my limits, to my spirit.

And perhaps most painful of all, pain taught me surrender.

Letting go of deadlines, expectations, and relentless pressure isn't surrender; it's a different kind of release.

The kind of surrender that allowed me to find new dreams, smaller, quieter, but no less meaningful.

Go Back and Get it

Parts of my life still show the scars of stolen years.
Projects I had to abandon.

Journeys I had to delay.
Plans I had to put on hold.

But there are also parts of me that could only be born through that fire:
The deeper compassion.
The patience with myself.
The gentler, fiercer kind of resilience that doesn't shout, but vibrates beneath my skin.

Pain broke me open.

But it also built something inside me that nothing, and no one, can take away.

Pain's lessons, though expensive, are my most precious.
Pain taught me that stillness is not failure.
And even in the stillness, my spirit can soar.

The wilderness years stretched before me, long, hard, silent.

I lost money.
I lost dignity.
I lost the ability to dream the way I used to.

Chapter 11:
IN THE WILDERNESS

For ten years, I fought a private battle few could see. Yet, God's voice resounded amidst my desolation and ruin.

I encountered the ancient African principle of **Sankofa**:

> "It is not wrong to go back for that which you have forgotten."

Maybe, just maybe, I hadn't lost everything.

Maybe the dreams, the gifts, the strength, were still there, waiting.

If I was willing to reach back, to go back and get them.

My illnesses didn't just take my energy; they stripped away my very sense of who I was.

The ambitious, vibrant woman who built a career and nurtured her children with fierce love was disappearing.

I felt invisible, not just in body, but spiritually and financially.

Clients and colleagues who once respected me now disrespected me.

Some even snarled, "If you're disabled, you shouldn't be working."

Others accused me of pretending, as if the daily battle inside my body was a fabrication.

Tears became my companion.
Anxiety sat heavy on my chest.
Hopelessness whispered that my life was over.

Moments of sheer terror tempted me to quit on life altogether.

The pressure.
The betrayal.
The feeling that all I had given to others was forgotten.

But somehow, somehow, I held on.
By a thread.
By faith.
By the sheer stubborn refusal to let darkness have the ultimate word.

Part Three:
THE TURNING POINT

"I will restore to you the years that the locust has eaten.", Joel 2:25 (ESV)

Chapter 12:
WHISPERS FROM THE PAST

Even as my body stiffened, even as fatigue weighed down every step, there were still whispers from the woman I used to be.

In quiet moments, when I closed my eyes, I could almost see her; fit, agile, laughing, powerful.

My once vibrant body now felt like a stiff, immovable lump.
Sedentary.
Trapped.

And yet, inside, the spark had not died.
It flickered.
It whispered: *You are still here.*

Chapter 13:
LEARNING ABOUT SANKOFA

The principle of Sankofa became my lifeline. It taught me that going back to reclaim what was mine was not failure; it was wisdom.

I commenced the work of remembering.

- The dreams of the girl I used to be.
- The skills I had once mastered.
- The strength I had once drawn on.

It was difficult.
My mind was scrambled from illness and grief.
My confidence had been shattered by life and by people.

But I drew on something deeper: **my faith in God.**

I entrusted Him with my life, my broken dreams, my business, my finances, my children, my grandchildren.

I prayed through tears.

I prayed when there were no words.

I trusted that if God had brought me this far, He could bring me further still.

"Be anxious for nothing, but in everything by prayer and supplication, with thanksgiving, let your requests be made known to God."
Philippians 4:6, NIV

Chapter 14:
A NEW ERA

After more than thirty years of serving women and children, something unexpected happened: my business attracted men.

At first, it surprised me. For so long, my work had been grounded in nurturing, advocating for, and building services around the needs of women and families. It was part of my DNA, part of my healing and giving back. But steadily, more men began seeking my services. Not just a few, it grew until today, around 75% of my clients are men.

And with them came a distinct energy.

The men who collaborated with me brought a higher level of respect for the work I do. They valued my expertise. They recognised my experience. They didn't haggle; they didn't push boundaries, and they didn't ask for freebies.

They came ready to invest in themselves, in their dreams, and in the work we did together.

For the first time in a long time, my day-to-day work felt easier, lighter, even pleasurable. The atmosphere in the team shifted too, more relaxed, more confident, more valued. There was a sense of clarity, mutual respect, and calm ambition that I hadn't realised I was missing until it arrived.

But this shift didn't happen by accident.

It came after a hard-won decision to change my business approach.

After years of serving and watching a minority of my clients disrespect the value I gave, I realised something had to change, and it had to start with me.

I strategically raised my prices.

I became selective about who I accepted as a client.

I made a conscious decision to protect the value of my work, to attract people who were serious about investing. Not just money, but respect, commitment, and gratitude into the partnership.

And as I made those internal shifts, my external world shifted too.

Gone were the endless negotiations, the emotional labour of trying to convince someone to see the worth of what I offered.
Gone were the late-night doubts, the bending of my standards to please people who only ever saw what they could take.

Instead, I built a business rooted in mutual respect, clear boundaries, and a deep belief in the transformational power of the work we do.

The irony is not lost on me.
After years of battling feelings of unworthiness, after years of struggling to monetise my skills appropriately, it was when I demanded more that I finally received it.

By valuing myself more, I taught others to do the same.

This new era isn't just about money. It is about fair exchange.
It's about freedom.
It's about ease.
It's about walking in the fullness of the woman I have become, strong, wise, unapologetic.

I still serve. I always will.
But I serve from a place of strength now, not sacrifice.

I no longer have to battle to be seen or respected.

I no longer have to carry resentment under the weight of generosity that was not returned.

This chapter of my life is proof that we do not have to stay trapped in old patterns.
We can evolve.
We can demand more.
We can become the women our younger selves never dared to imagine.

I have entered a new era, and this time, I'm not just surviving.

I'm thriving.

Chapter 15:
THE CATALYST

The final breaking point came through another toxic relationship. I had once again sought love. Once again hoped for partnership.

But instead, I encountered control.

Disrespect.

Verbal abuse.

Aggression.

I fell into the relationship after 10 months of sleepless nights. I was grieving.

Grief has a way of turning the world upside down. When my assistant passed away suddenly, it felt as though the floor beneath me crumbled. She had been more than support; she was my right hand, my rhythm, my calm in the storm. Her loss created a silence I couldn't bear. But what I didn't expect was the way that grief would steal my sleep.

Go Back and Get it

At first, I thought it was just shock. I told myself, "It's the adrenaline. You'll rest soon."
But soon the days lost their shape. There were no mornings or evenings anymore. Only nights.

Nights of trying to sleep and failing.
Nights of pacing.
Nights of lying still but feeling like I was falling.
Nights of tears on the pillow.
Nights filled with memories of her voice, her messages, her presence.

I tried everything, herbal teas, magnesium, warm baths, sleep sprays. I turned the lights low. I played soft music. I switched off screens. I journaled. I prayed. I begged God for rest.

But sleep wouldn't come.

Sometimes I would give in and pour a glass of wine, hoping it would help me relax. Sometimes I would take an over-the-counter sleeping tablet just to knock myself out for a few hours. It worked once or twice but the moment I tried to rely on it, even that stopped working.

I dreaded bedtime.
Sleep, which once felt like refuge, had now become torment.

During the day, I was a shell of myself. Foggy. Slow. Strained. Grieving not only the woman I had lost, but now grieving my energy, clarity, and peace. Insomnia became its own kind of grief.

A mourning of normality.

People saw me online and assumed I was managing. I was not. I was functioning, but not living. My nights were filled with restlessness and silent screams. My days were filled with fatigue and pressure.

And the worst part of chronic insomnia is not just the tiredness, it's the **terror**.
The fear that it will never end. The panic that your mind will snap. The isolation of lying awake at 4am while the rest of the world sleeps peacefully.

But I kept going.

Some nights, I simply lay there and cried.
Some nights, I whispered scripture like a mantra, not to fix anything, just to feel God near.
Some nights, I surrendered the fight and just sat with my grief, letting the darkness say what it needed to say.

When I met him, it felt like I had found my sanctuary.

I fell asleep on a visit to him and slept the whole night. I didn't plan to stay but the need for sleep and comfort held me there.

Slowly, gradually and thankfully... the sleep returned. Not perfectly. Not consistently. But it returned.

Insomnia was one of the cruellest companions of my grief.

I was so grateful for the rest, the sleep, the restoration, that I clung to him and his home. His home became the place I could sleep.

The only place I wanted to sleep.

Until I didn't.

I was in his way.

Until I couldn't.

I had overstayed my welcome.

Although he didn't say it.

Although his words said stay.

The actions spoke to my soul, telling me to go.

He had whispered many a "I love you," and I loved him too. I cared deeply for him even before we met in person.

We had clung on to each other for too long. It wasn't working.

One day, after months of tension, I lay down exhausted at his home after months of working hard on my businesses.

Instead of compassion, he unleashed a tirade;
calling me lazy, using profanities, pouring hatred over my tired spirit.

He slammed the door as he left and in that moment, as tears streamed down my face, anxiety choking my chest, I saw clearly:

This was not love.
This was not what I deserve.

I disassociated for a moment, standing outside myself, and then vowed:

"I will not become what he is trying to make me."
"I will reclaim my life."

I Didn't See It at First

I didn't realise it was abuse. Not at first. There wasn't yelling or bruises, just this slow, disorienting confusion that crept into my days and nights.

I would ask a simple question,
"Did you enjoy yourself last night?"
It was genuine, even caring. But what followed wasn't an answer.

It was a torrent of deflection:
"Why are you always questioning me? I can't even go out without being interrogated. This is why I don't tell you things, because you always twist it into something it's not."
Before I knew it, I was explaining myself, defending words I hadn't meant as an attack. That's when I learned the term **word salad**. I had lived it more times than I could count.

Then came the **gaslighting**.
If I brought up something he'd said that hurt me, he'd deny it outright.
"I never said that. You're imagining things. You always take things the wrong way."

"Why are you trying to start an argument?"
Soon I started wondering if I *was* too sensitive. If maybe I was the problem.

The **stonewalling** was a silent cruelty. Long stretches of silence. No words, no eye contact, no warmth. I would try to bridge the gap, to bring us back to peace, but he'd shut down completely. I felt invisible.

And then there was the **projection**. If he was in a mood, he'd say I was being unstable. If he was cold, he'd accuse me of not giving him space. When he pulled away, it was somehow because I had "drained" him. I lost track of my own reality trying to manage his.

There was also **impatience**, sharp sighs, irritation when I moved too slowly, asked too many questions, needed comfort. The message was clear: I was a nuisance.

He criticised how I looked, my clothes, my hair, my makeup.
Too much. Not enough. Too loud. Too plain.
There was no tenderness, only control.

Affection faded to nothing. No care when I was ill. No warmth when I needed reassurance.

I was expected to **serve**, quietly, consistently, without needing anything in return.

It took me time to name it all.
But once I did, I knew:

This wasn't love.
This was survival in a slow erasure.

And I am not here to be erased.

The once sanctuary had become a prison.

Go Back and Get it

I reached out for help from friends.

Some believed me; others dismissed me.

I arranged counselling.

I booked an appointment two weeks ahead.

But before the appointment even came, another barrage of verbal abuse drove me to a final decision:

I left.

Not perfectly.

Not without fear.

But with fierce, sacred resolve.

The girl inside me, the woman I am, was reclaiming her place.

Chapter 16:
WALKING THE SANKOFA PATH

From the day I walked away, my healing became my mission.

I began counselling, peeling back layers of pain, lies, and trauma.

I started reading self-help and life stories, letting others' courage fuel my own.

I joined support groups, seeking the warmth of those who understood silent suffering.

I pushed myself to walk a little further each month.

Each step, each breath, was an act of rebellion against despair.

Routine massage therapy soothed my mind and body

I layered self-care into my life:
- Setting boundaries.

- Basking in beautiful sleep.
- Saying no.
- Resting unapologetically.
- Protecting my peace at all costs.

I worked fiercely on healing my **inner child**; the girl who had first learned to accept less than she deserved.

I cradled her, loved her, and promised her a different future.

Each week, I learned about myself; I answered my most fundamental questions, why do I take myself to places where I am abused? Why do I have so much empathy for others? Why am I so trusting over others' motivations? Why is the cycle repeating?

I was adamant that this cycle, this pattern, had to stop right here and right now.

The abuse, the shunning, and community blame were excruciating.

To some degree, they were right; I shouldn't have gone there. But I understand now my motivation. Social media is deceitful and is manipulated to portray a false reality.

I saw behind his mask

That living situation horrified me.

And through it all, I clung to God.

Every prayer.
Every whispered plea.
Every tear that fell into His hands.

I healed, step by trembling step, not by rushing, not by pretending, but by honouring the slow, sacred work of becoming whole again.

Sankofa was no longer just an idea.
It had become my way of living.

I was not starting again as a broken woman.
I was continuing as a **seasoned warrior**.

Stronger, wiser, and deeply rooted.

And when I celebrated my 57th, I was not surviving anymore.
I started to thrive.

Healing wasn't just about mending my body or rebuilding my dreams.
It was about learning to embrace my life, all of it, with open hands and an open heart.

Through every step of my Sankofa journey, one lesson became clear:

Acceptance is where true freedom begins.

Chapter 17:
NO REGRETS:
A Lesson in Acceptance

Fighting against the past.

Fighting against the losses.

Fighting against the reality of what was, and what is.

I sought to rekindle my first marriage after 27 years of separation, It did not work, we were complete strangers, going back to get what I had lost, was not a mistake it ended a lifetime of longing and created the final opportunity to let go, close that door and move forward.

I thought if I fought hard enough, I could rewrite history.
Undo the pain.
Change the outcomes.

But all that fighting only made me weary.
It only deepened the wounds.

Acceptance, I learned, is not giving up.
Acceptance is not weakness.
Acceptance is strength.

It is the strength to stand in your truth, without denial, without fantasy, and still choose to move forward with hope.

Acceptance allowed me to lay my battles down.

I no longer needed to punish myself for the choices I made, for the people who hurt me, for the things I could not control.

I chose, instead, to accept:

- That my life had unfolded exactly as it needed to for me to become who I am today.
- That every detour, every heartbreak, every illness had shaped me in ways comfort never could.
- That regret was a weight I no longer wished to carry.

I learned to look at my past with compassion, not shame.

I learned to bless the journey, even the hardest parts, because they taught me resilience, faith, and fierce self-love.

I learned to forgive myself.

And in that forgiveness, I found freedom.

There are no regrets now.

Only lessons.

Only gratitude.

Only the unwavering truth that **everything was preparing me for something greater**.

When you accept your life, truly accept it, you take back your power.

You stop being a victim of what happened.

You start being the author of what happens next.

Acceptance is not the end.

Acceptance is the beginning.

The beginning of peace.
The beginning of joy.
The beginning

Chapter 18:
THE GIFT OF PACE AND BEING STILL

There was a time when I believed that constant motion meant progress.

That running faster, working harder, pushing further was the only way to prove my worth.

Illness changed that.

Pain slowed me down, at first against my will, then, finally, by choice.

I learned that **being still is not weakness**.
It is wisdom.

In the stillness, I could finally hear my own soul.
In the quiet, I could finally feel what needed healing.

I realised that rushing was often a way to outrun my pain. When I slowed down, when I stopped, even for just a moment, I could finally meet myself with compassion instead of judgment.

Now, I move at the pace my soul needs.

Some days that means bold action.
Other days, it means sacred rest.

Both are holy.
Both are healing.

I no longer apologise for the pace my life requires.
I honour it.

Stillness became not my enemy, but my teacher –
showing me that growth happens not just in the movement,
but also in the moments we dare to pause, breathe, and simply **be**.

"Revelling in the Moments: Tuning In to Life Again,"

Healing taught me not just to survive –
but to **live deeply again**.

I learned to tune into my senses –
to revel in the simple, sacred moments that make life beautiful.

- The warmth of sunlight on my skin.

- The scent of fresh rain on the pavement.
- The sound of my grandchild's laughter echoing down a hallway.
- The taste of a favourite meal savoured slowly.
- The feel of a soft blanket wrapped around tired shoulders.

When you have faced loss, when you have brushed against despair, **you no longer take small joys for granted**.

You taste life differently.
You hear differently.
You feel everything more vividly.

I no longer rush through the gifts.
I linger with them.
I thank God for them.

The richness of life isn't found only in grand achievements or milestones.
It is stitched into every small moment we choose to notice.
Every breath we take with gratitude.
Every smile we allow ourselves to feel.

Revelling in the moments is not a distraction from life.
It **is** life.

And every moment, once truly lived, becomes a thread in the tapestry of healing and wholeness.

"Be still, and know that I am God," Psalm 46:10 NIV

Chapter 19:
THE POWER OF INTUITION

There is a voice inside us that whispers long before the world shouts.
For years, I doubted mine.
I looked for confirmation, for permission, for proof but what I really needed was to trust the still, quiet knowing within me.
The one that warned me, guided me, reassured me...
even when I didn't want to hear it.

That voice was my intuition.
And now I know:
intuition is sacred.

It's not just a "gut feeling."
It's the voice of your Spirit.
The wisdom of your body.

The knowing passed down through generations of women who survived, endured, and learned.

We are not taught to trust ourselves.
Especially not as women, and certainly not as Black women.
We are trained to second-guess, to apologise, to over-explain.

But intuition doesn't need explanation.
It doesn't need credentials.
It needs courage.

There were moments in my life, in relationships, in business, in motherhood, in health –
when something inside me *knew* the truth long before I had the evidence.

But I didn't always listen.

I stayed too long.
I gave too much.
I quieted myself so others could be louder.
And it cost me.

Now, I don't argue with my intuition.
I don't debate with my gut.
I sit still. I listen. I trust.

Go Back and Get it

You know more than you think you do.
Your body knows.
Your spirit knows.

Intuition is God's whisper - the voice of love, protection, and alignment.

And trusting it is an act of self-respect.
You don't need to be perfect.
You need to be present.
And you need to believe that the answers you've been searching for...
are already inside you.

Chapter 20:
THIS IS NOT ABOUT OTHER PEOPLE

One of the hardest lessons I had to learn and perhaps the most freeing was this:

My healing, my joy, my life, was not about other people.

It was not about how they lived their lives.
It was not about what they thought of me.
It was not about whether they understood my journey, approved of my decisions, or applauded my healing.

For too long, I carried the heavy burden of other people's expectations.
I measured my worth by their reactions.
I doubted my progress because of their opinions.

But healing taught me this simple, sacred truth:

Go Back and Get it

Other people's opinions are not my compass.
Other people's lives are not my blueprint.

My life is my own.
My pace is my own.
My healing is my own.

I no longer chase validation.
I no longer contort myself to fit other people's comfort zones.
I no longer explain my worth.

I live aligned with God's purpose for me not anyone else's preferences.

Freedom came when I stopped asking,
"What will they think?"
and started asking,
"What does my soul need?"

Freedom came when I stopped looking outward for permission,
and started looking inward for peace.

This is not about them.
It was never about them.

This is about the life God has called me to live
full, free, joyful, and unapologetically my own.

Chapter 21:
LEGACY IN MOTION

And now, it is all about legacy.
After years of building, struggling, surviving, learning, and rising, my focus has shifted.
It is no longer just about what I can achieve.
It is about what I can *leave behind*.

Through my businesses, my services, my publishing house, my training, and coaching, I am creating a living legacy, a blueprint that others can use to build their own dreams.

Everything I have learned, every skill I have refined, every scar that taught me a deeper truth, I now offer it freely to guide others on their journey.

It is not enough for me to climb alone.
My vision is to reach back, to lift others as I climb, to create a ripple effect that moves far beyond anything my own two hands could ever achieve.

I see legacy not just as a future concept but as something alive right now, in every conversation, every book published, every client coached, every community service launched.

I see it in the way my businesses create opportunities for others, editors, designers, writers, creatives, trainers, and leaders.

I see it in the way my clients grow, flourish, and then go on to serve others too.

The vision is simple but profound:
To share everything I know, my knowledge, my experiences, my strategies, my mistakes, my triumphs, so that those who come behind me do not have to start from nothing.
So that they can stand on my shoulders and reach higher, dream bigger, move faster toward the lives they deserve.
I am no longer driven by survival.
I am driven by contribution.

I want my life's work to be a seedbed for future leaders, authors, entrepreneurs, and change-makers.

I want to create a pathway for others, especially those who have been overlooked, underestimated, or told they are too broken to succeed.

Legacy, for me, is service at its highest level.

It teaches using not only textbooks and theories but lived experience.

It declares: **"I offer my knowledge, which cost me greatly, use it, and surpass it."**

It heals generations through narrative transformation.

Resilience, dignity, power, and compassion can coexist.

I move forward with deep gratitude, not bitterness for what it took to get here, but gratitude for the strength it built in me.

Gratitude for the wisdom pain could never steal.

Gratitude for the love, faith, and community that held me together when the world tried to tear me apart.

This new chapter of my life is not the end of the road. It underpins something greater than myself, a legacy growing daily, built word by word, life by life.

I am planting seeds I may never see bloom.

And that, to me, is success.

Part Four:
FOR THE READER:
Your Sankofa Journey

"Be strong and courageous. Do not be afraid; do not be discouraged, for the Lord your God will be with you wherever you go.", Joshua 1:9 (NIV)

Chapter 22:
LESSONS LEARNED ALONG THE WAY

If there is one truth my journey has taught me, it is this: **Healing is not a straight line.**

It is messy.
It is painful.
It is slow.

But it is also beautiful.
It is sacred.
And it is possible.

Here are the lessons I offer you from the other side of the wilderness:

- **You are not broken beyond repair.**
  Even if life has shattered your plans, even if you feel lost, God's grace and your resilience still hold you together.

- **Your past is not your prison.**
  It is your treasure chest, filled with gifts, talents, and strengths waiting to be reclaimed.

- **Small steps are sacred.**
  Healing happens inch by inch, one prayer, one journal entry, one boundary, one walk, one brave "no" or tender "yes" at a time.

- **Faith is your anchor.**
  God has been there all along, in the silence, in the tears, in the quiet victories you thought no one noticed.

- **You deserve your own love first.**
  No external validation can heal the places inside you that need your own care, your own kindness, your own fierce loyalty.

- **You are allowed to begin again.**
  At 36, 46, 56, 76, there is no expiry date on reclaiming your life.

Healing is not about pretending nothing bad ever happened. It's about remembering that *nothing bad has the power to define you permanently.*

Chapter 23:
WOMANHOOD
Sacred, Sensual, and Seen

There is more to being a woman than bearing children or working hard.

There is more to being a woman than pain, duty, or silence.

There is also the sacred.
The sensual.
The soft.
The aching, intimate, yearning parts of womanhood that don't always get spoken about, especially by women of faith.

But I will speak them here.

Because I believe that healing is not only for the body and soul — but also for the woman inside me who longs to be seen, touched, cherished, and desired.

The Sensual is Not Shameful

I've had lovers.

I've had husbands.

I've known passion's fire, closeness, skin-to-skin sacredness.

And I've also celebrated a cumulative total of **over 15 years of celibacy.**

A deeply personal decision. A spiritual vow.

A way of cleansing, committing, and honouring my body and my God.

Both seasons, sensuality, and sacred separation, are part of me.

And yet, there are moments when I still ache for intimacy.

Not just sex, but connection.

To be held.

To be touched.

To be kissed tenderly.

To be looked at like I matter... like I'm still beautiful, still soft, still worthy of love.

Is that too much to ask?

Body Image and Womanhood

I've battled with my body.
Illness. Surgery. Weight gain. Pain. Immobility.
I've stood in front of mirrors and tried to recognise the woman I used to be.

But even in those moments, I never stopped being a woman.
A whole woman.
A woman who feels.
A woman who longs.
A woman who sometimes wonders, *Have I become invisible?*

Not having a consistent partner, not living with a husband, at times, I've questioned my femininity.
I've wondered if I was lacking, if I was less than,
because I no longer had someone who would reach for me in the night.

Sometimes, I felt like I was no longer being seen as a woman, just a mother, a coach, a worker, a strong figure holding everything together.

But inside... I am still her.
The woman who longs to be caressed.
The woman who still finds joy in a soft fabric on her skin.

The woman who still smiles at the idea of a wet kiss and a hand-held.

Is It Wrong to Long?

No, it's not wrong.
It's human.

It's not worldly to want warmth.
It's not sinful to grieve for what was or dream of what could be.
It's not shameful to want closeness, intimacy, affection, even at 57 and beyond.

We were made to be touched.
We were made to connect.
We were made for pleasure – yes, even holy pleasure.

And if celibacy has taught me anything, it is this:

Desire is not evil.
It is energy.
It can be directed.
It can be honoured.
It can be offered back to God in sacred waiting.
But it must never be denied out of shame.

Being a Woman, Still

So here I am –
not married, not cohabiting, seldom held,
but still...

A woman.

A full woman.

A holy woman.

A soft, passionate, strong, vulnerable, tender, celibate, sensual woman.

And I'm learning that I don't need to be in someone's arms
to know that I am still worthy of affection.
Still worthy of romance.
Still worthy of love in all its forms.

Yes, I may ache for a hand in mine.

Yes, I may crave a little tenderness.

And yes, that desire matters.

But I also know:

I am never less of a woman in the waiting.

I am whole... even here.

Even now.

Even alone.

The Woman in Menopause

Menopause is more than a biological shift it is an emotional reckoning.

It sneaks in, sometimes with fire, sometimes with fog. It strips away certainty. Your body changes, your memory drifts, your sleep deserts you. You wonder where the woman you used to be has gone.

You grieve your youth not out of vanity, but out of longing. The tight skin, the quick energy, the effortless confidence. You used to walk into a room and know you were radiant. Now you wonder if you are invisible.

Your clothes fit differently. Your moods swing wildly. Your desire, once alive and vibrant, now feels like a flicker fighting against the wind.

And yet, deep down, there's still a woman full of wisdom, softness, and fire who wants to be seen, heard, and loved. Not for who she used to be, but for who she is becoming.

Menopause may feel like a slow goodbye.
But it can also be a sacred awakening.
An invitation to rediscover your worth beyond youth, and to embrace the beauty of your becoming.

You are not fading.
You are evolving.

Chapter 24:
DREAMING OF MY SOFT GIRL ERA

There was a time I didn't believe softness was made for women like me.

I was built for resilience, shaped by storms, and praised for how much I could endure. Strength became my identity. But deep down, I longed for something different, a life that wasn't about pushing through or holding it together for everyone else. I longed for tenderness, gentleness, quiet mornings, emotional safety. I longed to exhale.

I was once described as *"a brick"* by the psychiatrist treating my ex-husband on a secure mental health ward. It was said with respect – I had stayed strong when many would have collapsed – but I remember how cold and weighty the word felt. I didn't want to be a brick. I wanted to be soft. I wanted to be held.

Being strong because you have to be is very different from being strong by choice. The version of strength I lived in stripped away my femininity. It hardened the edges of my voice, my body, my energy. Over time, I stopped expecting comfort, nurture, or protection. I didn't stop wanting it, but I silenced the longing.

Now, I dream of what I call my *Soft Girl Era*.

The world sees this trend online, soft lighting, flowers, luxury spa days. But for me, it's not about Instagram aesthetics. It's about finally allowing myself the gentleness I've denied. It's about rest without guilt. Love without performance. Beauty without burden. It's about sitting in the sunlight without explaining why I'm not doing more.

My Soft Girl Era is one of ease, not laziness, but *peace*. It's the healing balm to years of burnout.
It's the warm bath after the long war.

I no longer want to be the woman who grits her teeth and says, "I'll manage."
I want to be the woman who says, "I'm tired," and is met with kindness.
I want my home, my calendar, my relationships to feel safe.
I want softness in the way I talk to myself.

Softness in how I handle my body.
Softness in how I allow God to hold me.

Sometimes I dream not of applause or admiration but of help. Of real, quiet help.
Of being cherished, understood, and cared for.

Like *Andrex tissue*, I've been soft and strong all my life, but now I want to live in the softness, not hide it behind utility.

This is not indulgence.
This is healing.
This is me, finally, being the woman I was always meant to be.
My Soft Girl Era is sacred.

And I'm stepping into it, fully, faithfully, and free.

AFFIRMATION:

"I am allowed to be soft and strong. I release the pressure to prove, perform, or push. I honour my need for peace, pleasure, and protection. My softness is my sacred return to self."

Prompts for Journal page:

- How has being "strong" served me in the past? How has it harmed me?

- When was the last time I felt truly safe, rested, and held? What made that moment possible?

- What would a soft day look like for me - physically, emotionally, and spiritually?

- What beliefs do I carry that make me feel guilty for resting or receiving care? Where did they come from?

- How can I welcome softness into my daily routine, even in small ways?

Chapter: 25:
MY DILEMMA

Eleven years ago, I made a decision I believed would improve my life.
I was offered what was described as the "gold standard" solution for bladder dysfunction.
a 20-minute operation to fit a pelvic mesh.
A simple fix. Quick. Routine.
Sold to me with confidence and a promise of relief.

And I grabbed it.
Because I trusted the professionals.
Because I believed in solutions.
Because I wanted to get on with my life.

What was meant to be a solution became a sentence
a long, painful journey of illness, inflammation, nerve pain, exhaustion, and confusion.
Doctors dismissed it.
Tests showed nothing.
But I knew something was wrong.

Over time, the truth began to surface:
The mesh was eroding through my body.

Quietly. Relentlessly.
Causing damage, distress, and deep disruption to my health and wellbeing.
Over the past two years, the pain intensified as the device still inside me began to literally force its way out.

The Truth Behind the Mesh

This is not just *my* story.
This is part of a wider, global health scandal; where women around the world have been fitted with pelvic mesh devices without proper understanding, consent, or long-term care.

Many, like me, were poorly advised.
Many have suffered in silence.
Many have lost their health, their strength, their joy.
All because of a decision made in trust... that led to trauma.

Now, over a decade later, I am preparing for major surgery to have the mesh removed completely.
A procedure far more complex and serious than the one I signed up for.

This decision has not come lightly.
It has taken:

- Prayer
- Research
- Long conversations
- Tears
- And above all, faith

Because **the very thing that was supposed to help me... is now trying to leave my body uninvited and violently.**

Another Sankofa Moment

This, too, is Sankofa.

I am going back to face the very thing that threatens to derail my health.
I am not running from it. I am facing it head-on.
I am reclaiming my right to heal, even if it means enduring more pain in the short term.
I don't place my faith in the health system.
But I do place it in God, in His healing, His justice, His restoration, and the journey He is leading me on.

This chapter of my life is not easy.
But it is necessary.

To heal, we must confront past pain, understand it, and take back control.

To the Woman or Man Reading This

If you've ever decided in trust, that turned into trauma – I see you.

If you've ever been failed by a system, ignored in your pain, or left to carry the consequences of someone else's advice, I stand with you.

And if you are facing a decision now that feels terrifying but necessary,
I encourage you:

Pause.
Pray.
Research.
And trust your body, your wisdom, and your faith.

You have the right to heal.
You have the right to return.
You have the right to go back and get it.

Chapter 26:
A CALL TO ACTION,
Start Your Sankofa Journey

If something inside you is stirring,
if you are feeling the whisper, the tug, the ache, **listen.**

You are not imagining it.
You are being invited to begin again.

Here's where you can start:

- **Reflect on your past with love, not shame.**
  Go back and gather your gifts, your strengths, your victories.
  Write them down. Celebrate them.

- **Take one small step.**
  Book the counselling session.
  Join the support group.
  Enrol in the course.
  Write the journal entry.
  Walk the extra steps.
  Say yes to yourself.

- **Surrender the timeline.**
  Healing is not rushed. Growth is not microwaved.
  Trust God's timing. He is never late.

- **Surround yourself with life, givers.**
  Find the friends, mentors, communities who see your light, not just your wounds.

- **Pray boldly.**
  Pray even when your voice trembles.
  Pray even when you don't have the words.
  God hears the groanings too deep for words.

You do not have to see the whole path.
You only need to take the first step.

And when you stumble, because you will
fall toward grace, not guilt.
Fall toward healing, not shame.

You are not behind.
You are right on time.

Chapter 27:
IT IS NEVER TOO LATE

At 56, I chose to reclaim my life.
And I am still choosing it, every day.
You can choose too.

It is never too late.

It is never too late to gather your scattered pieces and build something beautiful with them.
It is never too late to heal the child inside you and honour the person you are becoming.
It is never too late to thrive.

Your past is not a life sentence.
Your pain is not your whole story.
Your setbacks do not cancel your calling.

Sankofa teaches us that what was lost is never truly gone.

It is waiting, patiently, faithfully, for us to go back and retrieve it.

Everything you ever had
Every gift.
Every dream.
Every ounce of courage.
Every drop of purpose **is still yours.**

Waiting.
Ready.
Yours for the taking.

You are not too broken.

You are not too old.

You are not too late.

You are exactly where you are meant to be to begin.

The best of your life is not behind you.

It is ahead.

It is now.

And it is yours.

Closing Reflection:
YOU COME FIRST

Dear one,

If you take nothing else from these pages, take this:

You come first.

Your healing comes first.
Your peace comes first.
Your joy comes first.

Your love for yourself must come first –
before the demands of others,
before the noise of the world,
before the pressure, to prove your worth.

You are deserving of love –
not just from others,
but from yourself.

You must apply that truth first and fiercest to your own heart.
You must speak to yourself with tenderness.

Go Back and Get it

You must nourish your own spirit with the same fierce loyalty you so willingly poured into others.

Only you, with the grace of God, can save yourself.

Only you can say yes to life again.
And when you do
when you gather the courage to reach back and fetch what is yours
the richness of life, the peace that surpasses understanding, and the deep, sustaining joy will meet you right where you are.

Everything you ever had –
every gift, every hope, every ounce of strength –
is still yours.

Waiting.

Ready.

Yours for the taking.
So go back, beloved.
Go back and get it.

YOUR GO BACK AND GET IT JOURNEY

A Guided Journal to Reclaim Your Life, Dreams, and Power

WELCOME TO YOUR JOURNEY.

This is your sacred space –
to reflect, to heal, to dream, and to rise.

There is no right or wrong way to walk this path.
There is only honesty, courage, and grace.

Take your time.
Write your truth.
Celebrate every small step forward.

This is your story now.

GO BACK.
GET IT.
LIVE IT.

HOW TO USE THIS JOURNAL

Dear Reader,

As you reach this part of *Go Back and Get It*, I want to honour you for coming this far.

This journal is a sacred space for you — to reflect, to dream, to heal, and to grow.

It's acceptable to use these pages in any way.

You are invited to:

- Take your time.
- Write as little or as much as you feel led.
- Pause and come back when you need to.
- Be honest with yourself, tenderly, bravely.

Some days, you may feel ready to pour out your heart. Other days, you may just sit with a single question in

silence.

Both are powerful.

You do not need to rush your healing.
You do not need to judge your pace.

This journal is yours.

Your journey.
Your truth.
Your becoming.

Breathe deeply.
Pick up your pen.
And trust the path ahead.

You are exactly where you need to be.

GOING BACK TO MOVE FORWARD

Reflection: Sometimes we must look back, not to stay there, but to gather the wisdom and treasures we left behind.

Journal Prompts:

- What passions, dreams, or gifts from your younger self have you forgotten?

_____
_____
_____
_____
_____
_____
_____
_____

- When did you feel most alive, curious, or brave?

- What would it feel like to go back and reclaim one of those parts of you?

HEALING WOUNDS WITH LOVE

Reflection: Healing begins with seeing, and loving, the wounded places inside us.

Journal Prompts:

- What wounds from your past still whisper doubt or fear into your heart?

_____
_____
_____
_____
_____
_____
_____
_____
_____
_____
_____

- How can you begin to offer yourself compassion instead of criticism?

_____
_____
_____
_____
_____
_____

- What does forgiveness (of yourself or others) mean to you today?

_____
_____
_____
_____
_____
_____
_____
_____

ACCEPTANCE AND FREEDOM

Reflection: Fighting life exhausts us.
Accepting life frees us.

Journal Prompts:

- What parts of your story have been hardest for you to accept?

_____
_____
_____
_____
_____
_____
_____
_____

- How might your life change if you fully embraced them?

- What would freedom feel like for you?

LISTENING TO YOUR INTUITION

- Think back to a moment when your intuition tried to speak to you.

_____
_____
_____
_____
_____
_____
_____
_____
_____
_____
_____
_____
_____

- Did you listen or ignore it? What happened?

___

- What would trusting your inner voice look like now, in this season of your life?

___

MY SILENT PAIN

- What pain have I been carrying silently?

_____
_____
_____
_____
_____
_____
_____
_____
_____
_____
_____
_____
_____
_____
_____
_____

- What decision have I delayed out of fear — even though I know it's time to act?

- What does healing look like for me, today?

- Use this space to reflect honestly and lovingly.

_____
_____
_____
_____
_____
_____
_____
_____

FINDING JOY IN SMALL MOMENTS

Reflection: Joy isn't hidden in milestones; it's woven into daily life.

Journal Prompts:

- List 5 simple things that bring you joy today.

___
___
___
___
___
___
___
___
___
___
___
___

- How can you intentionally savour one small moment each day?

_____
_____
_____
_____
_____
_____

- When did you last feel fully present?

_____
_____
_____
_____
_____
_____
_____
_____
_____
_____

RELEASING OTHER PEOPLE'S OPINIONS

Reflection: Your life is not a performance for others. It is a sacred unfolding of your own soul.

Journal Prompts:

- Whose approval have you been seeking, and why?

_____
_____
_____
_____
_____
_____
_____
_____
_____

- What beliefs about yourself can you reclaim today?

- How will you protect your peace going forward?

WOMANHOOD

- Have you ever denied your desire out of shame or fear?

- In what ways have I been silencing or suppressing parts of my womanhood, physically, emotionally, or spiritually?

___

- What would it mean for me to reclaim joy, sensuality, and sacred love on my own terms, at this stage of my life?

___

- Where in my life do I desire tenderness, and how can I give that to myself first?

_____
_____
_____
_____
_____
_____
_____

- What would it look like to honour your womanhood – body, mind, soul, and spirit, with love?

_____
_____
_____
_____
_____
_____
_____

I am not too old.
I am not too late.
I am not too much.
I am not not enough.

I am a woman.
Sacred.
Sensual.
Seen.
And wholly loved by God.

Remembering Your Dreams

Reflection: Dreams are not childish. Dreams are callings.

Journal Prompts:

- What dream have you hidden away, and why?

_____
_____
_____
_____
_____
_____
_____
_____
_____
_____
_____

- What small first step could you take to honour that dream now?

___

- What would your life look like if you trusted that dream again?

___

- When was the last time I felt truly safe, rested, and held? What made that moment possible?

  _____
  _____
  _____
  _____
  _____
  _____
  _____

- What would a soft day look like for me, physically, emotionally, and spiritually?

  _____
  _____
  _____
  _____
  _____
  _____
  _____

- What beliefs do I carry that make me feel guilty for resting or receiving care? Where did they come from?

_____
_____
_____
_____
_____
_____
_____

- How can I welcome softness into my daily routine, even in small ways?

_____
_____
_____
_____
_____
_____
_____

YOUR SANKOFA DECLARATION

Reflection: You are worthy of reclaiming everything beautiful, powerful, and sacred in your life.

Activity: Write your own personal declaration:

"I, _____, choose to go back and get it.
I reclaim my gifts / dreams / strength / peace / purpose
I walk forward with courage, faith, and joy.
My story is not over, It is still being written."

My Declaration:

YOUR JOURNEY CONTINUES

The journey is never really over.
Every day you choose healing,
every day you honour your dreams,
every day you show up for yourself with love,

you are going back and getting it again.
You are gathering your strength.
You are reclaiming your gifts.
You are rising with grace and courage.

Carry this truth with you always:
Everything you ever had is still yours.
Everything you ever dreamed is still possible.
And the best is yet to come.

You are living your Sankofa journey.

"I release shame.
I honour my pain.
I choose to heal, body, mind, and spirit.
I go back, not to stay there...
but to reclaim what is mine:
wholeness, strength, and peace."

"Healing is a journey without a map, but wisdom lights the path.

These books have offered light along my own journey.

I pray they bless yours too."

FURTHER READING

Recommended books and resources for your healing, empowerment, and Sankofa journey.

Healing and Personal Growth

1. The Body Keeps the Score by Bessel van der Kolk
   Understanding how trauma lives in the body and how healing can begin.

2. The Mother Wound: How to Heal Yourself and Transform Your Life by Bethany Webster
   A deep exploration of how early wounds impact our adult lives – and how to heal with love and truth.

3. Father Therapy by Kathy Rodriguez
   Healing the deep emotional impact of absent, abusive, or neglectful father figures – and reclaiming wholeness.

4. Let Them Theory by Mel Robbins
   An empowering approach to setting boundaries, releasing control, and trusting the flow of life.

5. It's OK That You're Not OK by Megan Devine
   Permission to grieve, heal, and live authentically through deep loss and change.

Faith and Spiritual Healing

1. Becoming by Michelle Obama
   A powerful memoir about identity, growth, resilience, and stepping into your true self.

2. The Purpose Driven Life by Rick Warren
   A Christian classic on finding meaning, direction, and purpose through faith.

3. Wholeness: Winning in Life from the Inside Out by Touré Roberts
   Healing inner wounds to live fully and purposefully.

4. Divine Alignment by Rhonda Santucci
   Aligning your life with divine purpose and rediscovering God's plan for your healing and success.

Empowerment and Reclaiming Dreams

1. Year of Yes by Shonda Rhimes
   How saying "yes" to self-love, healing, and courage changed everything.

2. Untamed by Glennon Doyle
   Breaking free from expectations to live authentically and fiercely.

3. You Are Your Best Thing edited by Tarana Burke and Brené Brown
   A powerful anthology centering Black voices on vulnerability, shame, and resilience.

Cultural and Ancestral Wisdom

1. Sankofa: Learning from the Past to Build the Future by M.J. Fievre
   Personal reflections on embracing identity, history, and empowerment.

2. Homegoing by Yaa Gyasi *(fiction but powerful)*
   A stunning novel tracing the intergenerational impact of history on healing and identity.

RESOURCES AND SUPPORT

🛠 Resources & Support for Pelvic Mesh Survivors

If you or someone you love has been affected by complications from pelvic mesh implants,

please know that you are not alone. There is help, information, and support available.

Here are some places to start:

- **Sling The Mesh (UK):**
  A patient support group campaigning for women affected by surgical mesh
  www.slingthemesh.co.uk
- **NHS Mesh Centre Information:**
  You can request referral to one of the NHS's specialist mesh removal centres
  Search "NHS Mesh Centre" + your region

- **Law firms handling mesh cases**
  (Choose carefully and prayerfully. Ask questions. Advocate for yourself.)

- **Support groups on Facebook and online forums**
  Many women are sharing their journeys, providing strength and community.

Depression and Emotional Distress

Depression can feel like a fog that never lifts – but healing is possible.
You are not weak. You are human. And you deserve support.

UK Support:

- **Mind – Free mental health information and helplines**
  www.mind.org.uk

- **Samaritans (UK) – 24/7 emotional support**
  Call 116 123 I www.samaritans.org

- **Black Minds Matter UK – Culturally competent therapy for Black individuals**
  www.blackmindsmatteruk.com

Facebook Support Groups:

- Depression Support Group (Worldwide)
- Women of Colour Mental Health Circle

Fibromyalgia

Fibromyalgia is real. It is painful, exhausting, and often invisible – but you are not imagining it. You deserve care, support, and rest.

Support Resources:

- **Fibromyalgia Action UK**
  www.fmauk.org
- **UK Fibromyalgia Magazine & Forum**
  www.ukfibromyalgia.com

Online Communities:

- **"Fibromyalgia Support & Advice"** (Facebook)
- **"Fibro Warriors"** (Instagram & online)

Trigeminal Neuralgia

Often called the "suicide disease," Trigeminal Neuralgia causes excruciating facial pain. It can be deeply isolating – but there are others who understand.

Resources:

- **Trigeminal Neuralgia Association UK (TNA UK)**
  www.tna.org.uk
  Helpline: 0800 999 1899

- **Facial Pain Association (USA-based but helpful worldwide)**
  www.facepain.org

Online Support:

- **"Living with Trigeminal Neuralgia"** (Facebook Group)
- **TNA UK Forum**

Diabetes (Type 2)

Managing diabetes is about more than medication – it's about lifestyle, awareness, and emotional support. With the right care, you can thrive.

UK Resources:

- **Diabetes UK – Trusted information, recipes, lifestyle help**
  www.diabetes.org.uk
- **NHS Diabetes Advice Line**
  Ask your GP to refer you for local support services

Online Support Groups:

- **"Type 2 Diabetes Support Group (UK)"** (Facebook)

- **"Black Diabetics UK"** (Instagram/Facebook)

Pelvic Organ Prolapse (Cystocele & Rectocele)

Pelvic organ prolapse (POP) occurs when organs like the bladder (cystocele) or rectum (rectocele) shift downward into the vaginal space due to weakened pelvic floor muscles. This condition can cause discomfort, urinary issues, pain, and a deep sense of frustration or loss.

You are **not alone** – and there is support available.

UK Resources:

- **Pelvic Organ Prolapse Support Association (POPSA UK)**
  www.pop-uk.org

- **NHS Pelvic Health Clinics** - Ask your GP for referral

- **The Pessary Project** - Education about non-surgical support options
  www.thepessaryproject.org

Online Communities:

- **"Pelvic Organ Prolapse Support (Worldwide)"** (Facebook Group)

- **"Living with Cystocele & Rectocele"** (Facebook)

- **Instagram:** @popuplifting and @pelvicroar

ABOUT THE AUTHOR
Marcia M. Spence

is a memoir writing coach, publisher, and passionate advocate for healing through storytelling.

After a lifetime of building, nurturing, surviving, and overcoming, Marcia found the courage to go back and reclaim the dreams and gifts she thought illness and hardship had stolen from her.

At the age of 56, she chose to believe that it was not too late, not too late to heal, to thrive, and to live fully.

Through her own powerful journey of chronic illness, loss, abuse, faith, and ultimate restoration, Marcia now inspires others to rediscover the strength, purpose, and beauty hidden in their own life stories.

She believes fiercely in the principle of **Sankofa**, that it is never wrong to reach back, gather what was lost, and move forward in wisdom.

Marcia lives her message daily: that everything you have ever needed is already within you, waiting to be reclaimed.

She continues to coach, publish, teach, and walk in the deep joy of a life redeemed.

Part Five:
CONTINUING YOUR JOURNEY

READY TO CONTINUE YOUR JOURNEY?

If this book has stirred something in your heart if you are ready to go deeper, heal further, and reclaim your life fully —
I would love to walk alongside you.

1:1 Coaching, Personalised transformational support

Group Programmes, Healing, connection, and empowerment in a community

Speaking Engagements, Inspiring talks for your conferences, organisations, or events!

Let's continue your journey together.

Contact me to find out more:

🌐 marciampublishinghouse.com
📧 marcia@marciampublishing.com

It's never too late to go back and get it.

Do You Really Want a Coach?

So, let me ask you a question —
Do you really want a coach?

Because a coach won't *save* you.
But she will remind you that you can save yourself.
She will hold up a mirror and show you what's still inside you... the dreams, the gifts, the brilliance, the courage you forgot you had.

But first, you have to want it.
You have to be willing.
You have to decide: **I am ready.**

Do You Value Coaching?

Coaching is not a luxury.
Coaching is a lifeline for those ready to step into their next chapter with clarity, strength, and direction.

The question is not *can you afford it*.
The deeper question is;

Can you afford not to change?
Can you afford to keep living under your potential?
Can you afford to stay where your soul no longer fits?

What Investing in Yourself Looks Like

Investing in yourself is not just about money.

It's about attention.

It's about time.

It's about intention.

It looks like:

- Showing up for yourself even when no one else claps
- Taking one brave step toward the life, you really want
- Asking for support instead of suffering in silence
- Saying, "I matter. My healing matters. My dreams matter."

And yes
it also means being willing to put money behind your healing, your growth, and your transformation.

Because when we value something, we make room for it.

We don't wait for permission, we prioritise.

The Outcomes You Can Expect

When you work with me, in any form, you can expect:

- ☑ A safe, confidential space to unpack your truth
- ☑ Deep inner clarity about what's holding you back
- ☑ Practical tools and guided support to move forward
- ☑ Accountability with kindness
- ☑ A real, soul-level transformation that doesn't just change your goals. It changes your life

But most of all, you'll begin to trust your own voice again. And that is priceless.

Coaching for Every Season

And Every Budget

Not everyone is in the position to invest in 1:1 coaching. I understand that.

That's why I've designed the **Go Back Get It Coaching Experience** to include:

One-to-One Coaching – deep, personal, transformational
Group Coaching Programmes – powerful collective healing
Online Self-Guided Coaching – flexible, affordable, still impactful

Because transformation should be available to every woman not just the wealthy.

No matter where you are in your journey there is a way for you to begin.

So... Do You Really Want a Coach?

Only you can answer that.
But if something stirred in you while reading this...
If your heart whispered, *"I'm ready,"*
Then I invite you to take the next step.

It's about remembering who you are and having someone walk beside you while you rise.

Join the Go Back and Get It! Movement

THE SANKOFA
LIFE AND CAREER TRANSFORMATIONAL COACHING PROGRAMME

Bonus Chapters
CRUCIAL WISDOM GAINED THROUGH SANKOFA!

Bonus Chapter
BUILDING WHILE BREAKING
The Birth of a Publishing House

I never set out to build a publishing company. I set out to heal.

I had written my memoir, Geraldine's Pearl, a raw, brave, healing work. My first serious writing. I was still recovering from depression, trigeminal neuralgia, and deep emotional exhaustion. The launch had given me a spark. The tour had ignited a flame. And then, something unexpected happened:

The floodgates opened.

My inbox filled. My messages exploded. My phone rang day and night. Aspiring authors, women, and men were reaching out to me, asking for help, for guidance, for a way to tell their stories and publish their books.

And I listened.

I didn't have a business plan. I didn't have seed funding. But I started a journey with no idea where it was leading me.

What I had was pain in my body. 27 tablets a day, braces on my back and hands, a brain that refused to give up, and a calling I couldn't ignore.

I struggled to move most days. My hands were wrapped in support bandages. My back braced. I sat on cushions and adaptive chairs just to stay upright at the computer.

But my mind? My mind was alive.

I was burning with ideas, strategy, creativity, and determination. So, I showed up.

Through tears. Through nerve pain. Through moments of despair.

I held Zoom meetings with clients while silently enduring excruciating pain. I hosted workshops between doctor visits. I sent invoices while massaging numb fingers. And every book I helped bring into the world... as The Authors' Midwife felt like it was keeping me alive.

I had no capital. What I had was my disability benefit, and I used it to build something greater than myself.

I invested in freelance editors, designers, and typesetters, relying on their goodwill and my ability to direct them. There were weeks we couldn't afford tools, software, even basic admin, but somehow, we kept going.

God sent help.

Always.

I transferred my skills, from social work, community leadership, management, and adapted them to a new industry. Publishing became my lifeline. My purpose. My ministry.

What started as one book, my memoir, became a movement.

I began with one author... then another... then ten. Soon, I was managing multiple full-scale publishing projects. nurturing writers, guiding healing stories to birth. We published books by all kinds of people, new authors, elders, and everyone in between. Every story was important.

Today, we've published over 300 books.

We produce a high-end magazine to amplify untold stories and build creative legacies. And every milestone has been made not despite my pain... but through it.

People see the end result, the glossy books, the magazine spreads, the author launches. But they don't always see:

The painkillers that kept me upright
The nights I cried silently between projects
The meetings I held while my body begged to rest
The invoices I sent while managing cash flow on a thread

The way I propped my business up using my personal income, not because I had to prove something, but because I believed in it that much

This wasn't a job. This was my purpose. My redemption. My Sankofa.

I was going back, through suffering, through struggle, to bring forward the gift that had always been in me. The ability to create, to connect, to birth, and to build.

This publishing house is not just a business. It is a sanctuary for stories. A place where forgotten voices rise. A space where purpose finds its pen.

And yes, I still live with chronic illness. Yes, I still face limitations. But my calling is limitless. And my faith has carried me where my body could not.

Reflection:

What dream have you delayed because you thought you had to be fully healed first?

What could you begin today, even with limited energy, support, or strength, that might bless your future self?

TAKE ON BOARD MY AFFIRMATION

I can build while breaking.
I can create in the midst of crisis.
I can serve through struggle.
I am not waiting to be perfect, I am walking in purpose.

Bonus Chapter
CURATING PEACE IN A SOCIAL WORLD

Social media has been both a window and a weight in my life.

It has allowed me to share my voice, promote my work, reach people I may never meet in person. It has helped me build my business, connect with my audience, and give visibility to the stories that matter.

But it has also been overwhelming. Draining. Loud.

At times, I've found myself scrolling for answers that only silence could give. Comparing my journey to the carefully curated lives of others. Feeling unseen despite being visible. Performing strength when I was exhausted. Posting joy when I was hurting. It became another mask, another platform where I had to "show up" – even when I was quietly falling apart.

There were days when I wanted to delete everything.
Days when I longed for obscurity.
But I knew my purpose didn't lie in disappearing, it lay in *redefining* how I show up.

Now, I use social media as a tool, not a mirror.
I no longer post for validation. I post from *alignment*.
I honour rest. I protect my peace. I set boundaries with my screen and my soul.

I remind myself: I do not owe the world constant access to my energy.
If I am quiet, it is not failure. It is *faithful rest*.

I can be visible *and* protected.
Present *and* private.
I can choose to share my story, not for attention, but for impact.

I am not here to perform. I am here to serve, softly, honestly, and without losing myself.

REFLECTION: Protecting Your Peace on Social Media
"I do not owe the world constant access to my life. My peace is more important than my presence online."

Journal Prompts:

1. How does social media make me feel most days? Energised? Drained? Inspired? Insecure? Why?

2. Have I ever found true friendship, love, or support through social platforms? What made those connections meaningful?

3. Where have I allowed access to people who don't deserve that space in my digital world? Who or what needs to be muted, unfollowed, or blocked?

4. Do I ever post to perform? To please? To prove something? What would it look like to post only from a place of peace?

5. What are my digital boundaries? Do I allow time away? Do I filter what I consume? How can I honour those boundaries better?

6. If social media disappeared tomorrow, how would I continue to express my voice, passion, and purpose?

AFFIRMATION:

"I am allowed to protect my energy. I release guilt about being unavailable. My digital space reflects my emotional space, calm, clean, and intentional."

Bonus Chapter
THE LONG ROAD TO PATIENCE AND FORGIVENESS

Patience was never my default. I was raised to move, to strive, to survive. Life didn't always allow me time to wait, so I pushed, persisted, and performed. But life, with its unpredictable storms, taught me what no book could: that some things take time. Healing takes time. Understanding takes time. Forgiveness takes even longer.

And not just forgiveness of others, but of *myself*.
I have had to forgive myself for what I didn't know.
For the choices I made while in survival mode.
For the times I gave too much or held back out of fear.
For the years when I wore strength as armour and didn't allow my softness to speak.
For believing I wasn't enough or too much for the wrong people.

Patience came slowly. It didn't arrive in quiet moments with candles and calm. It arrived in the chaos, in the ache of chronic pain, the tears that came at 3am, the prayers whispered through clenched teeth. It arrived when I had no choice but to wait on God.

And in that waiting, I learned: **forgiveness is a process**.
Sometimes it comes in layers.
Sometimes it starts with understanding.
Sometimes it starts with walking away.

I've forgiven people who never said sorry.
I've forgiven situations that will never make sense.
And I've made peace with the girl I once was and all the ways she fought for me.

Now, I walk slower.
I speak softer.
I respond with a little more grace, even when it's hard.

Patience and forgiveness haven't made me weaker.
They've made me wiser.

I still get it wrong sometimes.
But I no longer live in punishment. I live in **process**.
A process that looks more like freedom, and less like guilt.

This is the slow, holy work of healing.

And I am here for all of it.

REFLECTION: Patience & Forgiveness

"Forgiveness is not a destination. It is a decision I keep making every day, in every breath, with grace."

Journal Prompts:

1. Who or what have I been holding resentment toward, and how is that affecting my peace?

2. Have I truly forgiven myself for past choices or mistakes? What would self-forgiveness look like in action?

3. When was the last time I practiced patience with myself, with others, or with life's timing? What helped me stay grounded?

4. Is there someone I'm waiting on to apologise? What might it mean to release them, even without an apology?

5. How can I begin (or continue) the process of forgiveness while honouring my boundaries and my healing?

6. What does "living in process" mean to me? How can I make peace with the pace of my own growth?

AFFIRMATION:

"I forgive because I deserve peace. I am patient because I trust divine timing. I release guilt, blame, and shame, and choose to walk forward in grace."

Bonus Chapter
THE PIECES OF ME
Motherhood and Grandmotherhood

To say that being a mother is important to me is an understatement.

It is the most sacred role I have ever held. It shaped my womanhood, challenged my strength, expanded my heart, and broke me open in ways nothing else could. My children are grown now, living their adult lives. And I have three grandchildren, one now a teenager, and two more who continue to fill my heart in new ways.

When I look at them, when I really *see* them, I don't just see *their* lives. I see the **pieces of me**.

I see the way they speak with conviction, that came from me.
I see the way they navigate life with strength wrapped in grace, that's my doing.
And sometimes I see their wounds, their hesitations, their anxieties, and I know those came from me too.

Motherhood is not just about what I gave them. It's also about what they've shown me. Each child, in their own way, has held a mirror up to me, reflecting not only who I've been, but who I am still becoming.

Now, as a grandmother, or as I like to say, a *Glamma*. I occupy a different space. It's softer. Wiser. Still protective, but more spacious. I offer guidance with fewer words. I give love that doesn't chase or rescue, but *rests* and *welcomes*. I honour the rhythm of each generation. I watch my legacy unfold in the gestures, decisions, and dreams of the young ones.

And yet - oh, how I wished I had been well in the early years of their lives. I had dreamt of the fun we would have… the games, the adventures, the stories and songs. But my body didn't allow it. Chronic illness placed limits on what I could offer, and that truth quietly broke my heart.

Still, I know now… **it's not too late.**
Not too late to laugh.
Not too late to connect.
Not too late to pour into their lives with all the wisdom, creativity, and joy I carry now.
There is still time to give them memories rooted in presence, even if the past held pain.

I am a mother. I am a grandmother.
But above all, I am a woman watching her love move through time.
And that is the greatest gift of all.

JOURNAL REFLECTION: The Pieces of Me

"I am watching my love move through time, in the hearts of those I have raised, and those they are raising too."

Journal Prompts:

1. What does being a mother (or caregiver) mean to me at this stage in my life?

2. How do I see myself reflected in my children and grandchildren? What qualities or values have I passed on?

3. What do I grieve about the past in my parenting or grandparenting journey, and how can I show myself grace?

4. In what ways can I be present for my loved ones now, regardless of what I wasn't able to do in earlier years?

5. How do I define "legacy"? What would I love to be remembered for in my family line?

6. What moments, big or small, have reminded me that I've made an impact as a mother, Glamma, or matriarch?

AFFIRMATION:

"I honour the mother I was, the grandmother I am, and the woman I am still becoming. My presence is powerful. My love is timeless."

www.marciampublishinghouse.com

www.ingramcontent.com/pod-product-compliance
Lightning Source LLC
Chambersburg PA
CBHW010248010526
44119CB00055B/775